THE MAN

WITH ONE

SHOE

SURVIVAL AND RECOVERY:
LIVING BEYOND A SERIOUS MENTAL DIAGNOSIS

CHRISTOPHER COX

BALBOA
PRESS

A DIVISION OF HAY HOUSE

Balboa Press books may be ordered through booksellers or by contacting:

Balboa Press
A Division of Hay House
1663 Liberty Drive
Bloomington, IN 47403
www.balboapress.com
1 (877) 407-4847

Print information available on the last page.

ISBN: 978-1-5043-9052-1 (sc)
ISBN: 978-1-5043-9054-5 (hc)
ISBN: 978-1-5043-9053-8 (e)

Library of Congress Control Number: 2017916629

Balboa Press rev. date: 10/26/2017

"We can't direct the wind but we can adjust the sails"

Thomas S. Monson

UPON REFLECTION OF MY MINDSET during the time I first entered the psych ward in Little Rock, Arkansas, it occurs to me that perhaps I was on a journey to discover my truth. The truth is that I had chosen the wrong path; the path of ambition and wealth. Even at an early age I did have some success in seeking a way to overcome humble beginnings monetarily, but deep in my soul I understood that life was much more than money and prominence. Although I am the sixth of eight children, I was the first (and only) to join the military, the first to finish college and the first to live overseas. I somehow knew that life was a lot more than the harsh bubble that I had grown up with living in rural Mississippi and my eyes were widened to new possibilities when we moved to South Florida where I was introduced to many other cultures early in my life. I treasured the diversity of these distinct worldviews and seemed to develop a keen appreciation of all things unlike myself.

When I entered the military I again confronted this mixture of backgrounds and could blend my perception of reality to encompass all the influences from these diverse people. All this time, I conflicted with my formative years where I was sheltered from going near others who did not look or act as my family looked and acted. I now consider this a weakness on my part and have fought hard to overcome the bias I subconsciously possess against "others." Without genuine guidance concerning values and on interacting with people of other races, religions and cultures, I had to create my own reality that somehow got skewed into what became an unbalanced mind.

I know that biology played a major role in my abnormal thinking that left me in a padded room, but I also feel that environmental influences caused my distorted view of how life was supposed to be. I was not living the true path I needed to be on and I had to, "adjust my sails", in such a drastic way to correct my ship. Even though it took over 20 years to realize this correction of thought, it was well worth the effort. I was oblivious to what or why I was in this state of denial but the outcome of the peace I feel now made the journey worthwhile.

Presently working in the human services field, first as a volunteer for several years then making the switch to full-time employment, I believe I have found a calling; one where I can make a difference in other people's lives. I accept as truth that the principles of peer work correlate perfectly with the life lessons I have been educated in. We must be life-long learners and embrace diversity as strength both personally and institutionally. Other's cultures are part of our, "make-up", and as a community, should be cherished.

I remember at times during my search for wholeness, I would visit various organized religious communities never feeling acceptance or fulfillment in spirit. I honestly feel that my pendulum has swung from total confusion concerning matters of the heart to a place of approval within myself to have the confidence to rationally think in a healthy way relating to holistic health; mind, body and spirit. This transition did not come easily. When you are taught to fear Jesus at an early age, you tend to bow to whatever is accepted by the current trend of this time, however, if one truly has an open mind and can rationalize in a healthy way to not intrude on other's beliefs but come to an understanding of oneself and be comfortable in our own skin, this lets us fit in our community of choice allowing for the evolution of the acceptance we crave.

This book is a collection of thoughts that I possess after years of yearning. These are memories, as true as I know them to be. They may seem odd to the reader at times but so is an unbalanced mind!

The weatherboard

Upon entering the facility, I noticed a weatherboard. It was obviously old and weathered itself. On it was a date that was correct, the days of the week and little symbols that represented the type of weather outside for the day. Little rain drops as a symbol of rain, a sun for sunny, etc. It struck me as odd and outdated until I looked around the facility which was dark and miserable. There were no open windows of light, only fluorescent bulbs flickering. I saw this board as an indicator that this was a place to simply pass the time. This was a warehouse for the soul. I would find no answers here, just medication and idle time. Being maintained was the goal.

I had been here before, maybe not this ward but the same type of place. I grew to find these controlled environments as a vacation from the chaotic life I led on the outside, the real world where I was not appreciated or even tolerated. I had become a man with no true realistic thought process. Only visions of how life was supposed to be in my world - the world of Shamans and Visionaries. I felt there was a place for me and those like me. A serene existence for those of us that could find it but for now, I must undergo the life sucking concoctions of poisons they call medication; thorazenes, haldols, respidols and lithiums. These were the truths of my current state of being. At this point I was simply a statistic, a fraction of a whole, no one to be relied on or called upon for advice. Although I was a graduate of a respected institute of higher education, I had become only a part of a man. An insignificant individual that needed a weatherboard to tell me what the weather was. I could not be trusted with a window for God forbid I should jump out of it and end the misery I found myself in - time after time, hospital after hospital, psych ward after psych ward.

I had a curious mind. I would question life and its rules and regulations of today. Question who should judge and who had it right concerning reality. Was I so wrong as to have to be confined for only wanting answers to my personal quest for a holistic meaning in an unreal world? Sure, I had to be safe, not be a threat to myself or others but who were the ones saying I crossed this invisible line? The same ones that could not control their own lives! I did not blame the people - just the system. The system that says that "maintaining" is enough; to hell with what it means to be human. Why the hurry to lethargic medication? Let's numb the shit out of them and watch them pass the years in a fog. I applaud the doctor that agreed after my decade in this cloud to take me completely off the medication and let things take place naturally. Why I needed his permission is another consideration! I would cycle for several years but at least I felt sorrow, happiness, grief, hate, love. This was living! The consequences for my actions were steep but I was alive and made my own choices, let me live with them. I was but one in the system, some found comfort but I simply took a break from the universe and took a breath for a short period of time. I would then reengage the madness until the depression took me down again. I was beating my head over and over, deep down I knew there was an answer to this madness. Eventually I found it, the wise mind where emotion and logic overlap. The interlocking reasoning of the two worlds I had to walk in. The world of rules and coherent thought that is required in today's reality and the balancing of the other world, the one I found myself living in for over 30 years, and one where healers and sages thrive in mystery and pure energy. The world that transcends time and space, and the one that I believe is much more rational and logical than the first. It was this transformation of thought I was searching for all these years. I had found the key that allowed for that balance in life I yearned for. I began to live.

The early years

One would think when writing about their story the beginning would be the early years in that person's life but I find myself writing this chapter concerning these times last. I began my writings at the point in my life that I found to be the most life changing, that being when I had first entered the mental health system in Little Rock, Arkansas at the age of 28. As I look back over my childhood years there are moments that stand out for me that might give a clearer picture on my perspective of life and those environmental factors that influenced and intensified my mental health deterioration that lead me to be institutionalized so many times.

As I mentioned earlier, I am the sixth of eight children where seven of us were born in a single decade (no twins). This basically means that we were so close in age that we affected each other whether we wanted to or not. Being the middle son with four older sisters put me in the hierarchy somewhere between not mattering at all and being pampered to the extreme. I found this position well suited for me since I have always preferred the "backrow" in any situation and I appreciated the doting of my sisters. I could write of happy days filled with laughter and energy from all of us as children, always looking for ways to occupy our time and this was part of the truth of those days but to keep everything honest and truthful I must write my truth and that is a different story than that of some of my siblings.

Growing up in a small home with ten people is not easy on the best of days. We utilized the woods in the back of our home many times as a second bathroom and with three bedrooms the sleeping arrangements were challenging. We had money only when we could muster a few soda bottles for candy or found a yard to cut in the summer time. We all pitched in to make sure the bills were paid which is what one does in a democracy. My mother's natural wisdom was apparent to all that knew our family and she was the go to person to reason with my father and was the true leader of our clan.

I was aware of our economic status as I was growing up but this not affect me in a major way. I was also aware of the perceptions of other people outside our family concerning us since we put on such a front that most of what I remember was the way the Cox's were treated as a stalwart family to be admired. All children in the right place at the right time, all clean and dressed appropriately, all respectful and well mannered. Of course, all glass houses tend to break at some point and mine unraveled piece by piece over the years.

Looking back, I have always seen life in a sort of short piecemeal stories or in frame by frame visions. I would practically float through conversations, interacting appropriately but in the back of my mind I was always looking for the motive behind the action of others. What was their agenda and why are they doing what they do. When you view life in this manner you tend to find flaws and positive aspects in character quickly. To add to this mindset was that my memory had a way of filing even the smallest detail of an event so I would revisit conversations and interactions repeatedly until I somehow made since (in my mind) as to what had happened and why.

This way of reasoning is eventually what lead to my glass house crashing down around me.

I suppose the best example of this was how the constant influence of religion was pushed on us as an absolute way of life. I never understood the draw that organized religion has on people. I found it bothersome and time consuming with little or no purpose. I know this reads as though I have an ax to grind with those in positions of power within the churches we attended every Wednesday and twice on Sunday but it is much more basic than that. I have sat through probably a thousand sermons and I did find some nuggets of truth but for the most part it is being driven by a story that has been rewritten so many times that literally no one knows what the truth is! You throw guilt in and a little power struggle with people positioning for influence and there you have it; organized religion. This rational on my part was hard fought and I still bend at times to appease my parents just out of respect for them. So, I find that bowing my head and taking a moment to clarify my thinking is a small price to pay to not be in the trenches with the masses of people who attend and contribute to these organizations on a constant basis.

The local churches do a lot of good as far as feeding and sheltering the needy and as a person that works in the human services field I truly appreciate the efforts of these resources but for the most part my thinking takes me as far away from these organizations as I can get.

The next process of thinking I could never quite grasp is the idea that the color of one's skin matters! Having been brought up in Mississippi until approximately eleven years old, it was hammered into to me that white privilege was the norm and that was the driver of all socially acceptable behavior. I have found the opposite is true, that all cultures and races of people have much to contribute to our society and I am proud that I am fortunate to consider other people as fellow travelers in this world. What the hell difference does their life styles have to do with me when they are not intruding on my beliefs or life. This is also something I had to rationalize over time. Fortunately, I moved with my family to South Florida at an age where I could be positively influenced by others, other than the white canvas I was accustomed to.

For an individual who has a long history with mental health

systems, it might seem odd that I would be talking about rational thinking so much, but the working of society now and the irrationality that is common is the backdrop that set me up for a complete breakdown.

I saw life in black and white, what I had to come to grips with was the grey areas. When I attempted to stop drinking alcohol at 27 I could not function in what I saw as an unbalanced society when all along it was me that needed to change. Rules were for other people and if I did not tread on others I could think and act as I wished. This was irrational on my part and the change in myself that was needed to correct this mindset was a difficult lesson to learn.

When my thoughts ran rapid and I could not put two consecutive ideas together because of my biological condition and the cause of environmental effects, I simply melted into a state of madness.

As I grew into puberty I found that if I took certain steps I would be rewarded in a positive manner. I remember at the age of thirteen my desire to attract females was so great that I lost approximately 30 pounds in a single month, shedding baby fat rapidly. I had lost so much weight that my concerned mother took me to the doctor for a check-up. After a short exam, the doctor asked me if I had a girlfriend and my reaction told him all he needed to know. He smiled and told my mother that I was fine and that I was acting naturally. I learned from this that when I made my mind up I could accomplish some amazing feats, both physically and emotionally, I could influence people around me (girls mainly) with relative ease and this caused me to get into trouble more than I would have liked. I did play sports and was average but again I saw little need for competition and eventually quit them and began working a job at an early age. My first job that I can recall, where I received a check, was working for my father at his laundry plant. It was very demanding but I was a good employee and the work kept me in good shape physically. The next "regular" job I was employed at was the Burger Chief fast food restaurant. I do not remember how I obtained this job but I would work there off and on for the next two years, from the age of 15 to 17. I was a hard worker and became the night manager before I left after graduating high school.

School was something I never had any problems with academically, socially I found myself floating from click to click joining whatever group of people I found interesting at any given time. I went from hanging out with the jocks to mingling with the college bound to smoking weed with the surfers. I never quite fit into any group and this was fine with me. I only have one lasting relationship from those days.

I never gave much thought to what happened after high school so I was ill prepared to enter the work force and make my way into being an adult living on my own. My father got a job transfer back to Mississippi shortly after I had graduated so my living at home was ending abruptly unless I went to Mississippi with my parents. Being 18 at the time with no ties to Florida, I decided to follow them after a short period of time.

I did not realize just how out of sync I was from the people of Mississippi. Though segregation had been found unlawful many years before, for all practical purposes whites stayed in their communities and blacks stayed in theirs. There was an air of inequality that I had not encountered since my years living there as a young boy. I found this unacceptable then and now. The Mississippi "bubble of reality" I met unnerved me and therefore I rarely visit my relatives inside the state. It is a form of hate that is in my family's culture and this prejudice is destructive and unnecessary.

After arriving back in Jackson, I was approached by a brother-in-law who knew a man who worked in construction that I could work with. The job was as a trim carpenter. We basically finished the inside of new homes fitting them with cabinets, doors and molding. I would wake early, work a full day and be home by dark. I enjoyed being able to "stand back" and see what I had accomplished doing this work but after six months or so I knew I wanted more from my life than making low wages and working sunup to sundown. So, I got an education loan and started my secondary education at a junior college, living on campus.

All through these years of high school and into becoming a young adult I did drink and smoke marijuana but again those I associated with did the same so I thought at time that this was normal behavior but I seemed to do this to the extreme when I did partake with mind altering substances. I would go for weeks or months without anything then binge for short periods of time. I did do some irrational acts when I drank but except for being embarrassed I really did no harm to others or myself.

After a single semester in junior college I knew I could not keep up with working and maintaining school so I started looking for other options for my future and getting out of Mississippi. My roommate at the college was with the Army National Guard and had experience with the military. Although no one in my immediate family had served in the military I went to an Air Force recruiter, took the exam to enter and within a couple of months I found myself in Bootcamp.

The military gave me structure and purpose. Being mission oriented came easily to me so I adapted well. I was able to keep a since of self even when, with a shaven head, we all looked alike and shared the same like experiences. After Bootcamp, I was chosen to go to an electronic technology school for what was called Crypto Maintenance. I was in a class of approximately eight Airman. I did well in school and after 6 months or so I graduated and was sent to Langley AFB, Virginia to serve in the communication squadron. Again, I did well but my alcohol drinking increased dramatically. It was routine for us younger Airmen to spend several nights a week at the Noncommissioned Officer's Club or NCO club where the drinks were cheap and there were many women available for relationships.

After completing my follow-up studies and on-the-job training necessary to advance, I received orders to transfer to Germany to serve at the Sembach AFB for a two-year term. I had met a lady during my tour in Virginia and we were living together in her apartment for a short period of time. She was also an Airman who had been in service for several years longer than I. It was a chaotic few months we had together in Virginia but we grew very fond of each other. I left Virginia with heavy heart for this lady but the adventure of another country was so enticing that I put all aside and flew to Germany as scheduled.

I found Germany and the people of Dutch land simply wonderful. I moved off base with another Airman into a two-bedroom apartment in a small town a few miles from base. Bought a car for about $150.00 and quickly made many life-long friends both German and Air Force. The beer and wine were excellent and cheap on base and off so my habits were getting worse but I was a young man in a delightful place to be.

After a few months in Germany I started yearning for my relationship I had with the lady that I left in Virginia. I would go to the phone switch operators late at night and place free phone calls to the US through the military phone system and beg her to come to Germany to join me. She agreed and actually called the headquarters where new assignments were generated and talked her way into an assignment to Sembach AFB, the same small base I was stationed. Before she came she took a trip over to see me and we had a glorious two or three weeks to ourselves. We agreed that since she was coming to Germany that we should get married. The next few months were preparations for the wedding and her move to Europe.

On the week before the wedding I did what is called a "Hop" to England trying to eventually get to Virginia where we were to wed within a few days. To "Hop" basically means to catch a ride with a military airplane that is going wherever you want to go. The only catch is that the schedules for these planes are everchanging both in takeoff times and destinations. I would find this out first hand during my adventure back to the states for our wedding. When I arrived from Ramstein AFB, Germany to England, I was expecting to be able to catch a flight within a day or so to the states. Three days later I was still sitting in the air station I arrived at. I had very little money and was surviving on coffee. Finally, a C-130 that was heading for Dover AFB in Delaware was scheduled and we were allowed to board the plane. I called my fiancé from England letting her know I was getting on a plane, the number of the flight and the destination. After we boarded the flight plan changed to North Carolina and I had no way to warn her as she headed for Dover, Delaware. Needless to say, we had quite a time getting all straightened out but she found me in North Carolina and brought me home to Virginia where after a very long week we were married and I took a commercial flight back to Frankfurt, Germany.

My wife followed me shortly after and we spent the next four years or so by ourselves in Europe.

All during this time I continued to drink with my drinking getting heavier and heavier. I would do various unnormal acts while drinking that bordered on insanity. I did go to college at night and on most weekends, almost anytime I did not have to work and was able to earn a BS Degree. The pace I kept was frantic between school, work and home. I remember neglecting my wife during this time and it was all I could do to keep my schedule. By the end of the four years I was exhausted and by the time we came back to the states, I began making one bad decision after another concerning all aspects of my life. I was acting grandiose at one moment and crying the next. All the time drinking alcohol. My last six months of service was accomplished at Tinker AFB, Oklahoma. I was in such a mindset to get out of the service that the General in charge agreed to discharge me early with an Honorable discharge. It was best for all concerned! We gathered our belongings from where I had entered the Air Force in Jackson, Mississippi and took them back to Virginia.

Back to civilization

I was discharged from the United States Air Force thinking I had the world by the tail. I went in during 1980 as an enlisted airman and six years later I was perfect on paper. I had earned a B.S. degree in Business Management from the European division of the University of Maryland, completed a two-year degree in Electronic Technology from the Community College of the Air Force; maintained a high security clearance and put under my belt six years of specialized training on highly complex communication equipment that was in demand by the civilian market. Unfortunately, I also drank heavily, did irrational random acts (mostly covered up by my Air Force friends) and was my own worst enemy by not appreciating my loving wife during these years.

The later caught up to me in 1988 when I was working as a defense contractor. I soon realized that management did not appreciate my drinking so I attempted to quit my alcohol intake. I started making even more irrational decisions. Apparently, I had been self-medicating with alcohol for many years so when I stopped, my mind went to a place where I could not control my thinking. The mental illness was controlling me. Although at the time, I had no idea what was happening or how to "fix" me.

Even though I had worked for over eight years to establish

myself in the path I had chosen, I decided practically overnight that a change in career was needed. I moved my wife and me to another state (Mississippi) and tried to make a living as an office manager. During this time, I was as confused and frustrated as I could be and my mind was running rapid with wild thoughts. I was truly acting as a mad man with no rules or reason for my actions.

Driving Mad

I left my job in the middle of the day knowing I would never return. I was going to meet the president and advise him of how to proceed on several items of interest. As I was driving along I-20, a truck from the business I just left pulled up beside me and a friend rolled down the window and asked me where I was going. I yelled that I was going to meet the president. He looked at me with a puzzled look and continued down the road. My mind was racing. All my senses were on edge and I was manic to the point of dangerousness. I drove to my wife's work and had her pulled from her desk. She was confused on why I was there, but I assured her we had to leave immediately, to where I had no idea. Her employer allowed her to leave so we took off to a destination of a mad man. She kept asking me what was happening and why was I not at work. I told her that I could not explain to her all the details concerning my actions but all would be alright. I had been identified as a leader who had opportunities of holding political office. A senator for the state of Mississippi or possibly some other office but that I was sure I had been handpicked for greatness. I just could not explain everything to her for it was far too complex for her to comprehend. As we drove down I-55, I turned the radio to a volume that truly scared her. I was screaming over the music trying to explain my actions saying we

14

had to have the radio so loud to drown out our conversation since "they" were listening to our every word. I was bringing my wife into my world that I had been silent on for a long time. It was time for action and I was ready for the challenge! The entire time we had been in Mississippi we had been watched by adversaries and allies alike. There was a grand plan for me and my future but now was the time to act. To draw out those that were behind me and those that were not. It was logical to me that I should have been singled out. I was educated, had a background that was admirable and I was a product of Mississippi having been born in the city of Moss Point, on the coast. I was destined for high office. As I drove frantically around Jackson, I would speed up then slow down, roll my windows up then down, do whatever it took to throw "them" off my tail. My wife was holding on to her seat trying to rationalize to me that my actions made no sense but what did she know? She did not have the insight that I possessed! I was the one singled out and I had to do my part for the betterment of the world. We finally ended up in a strip mall where a church of sorts was located. I do not know exactly how we ended up there but after several of hours of driving, I think my wife was just relieved that we stopped. The doors to the church were open and a lady met us at the door. My wife was trying to explain to her that I was not feeling well when I felt the need to go further into the building. There were two men at an Alter and I approached them. I was thirsty and grabbed the only thing that looked as though it was consumable and that was the water in a ceremony cup they had placed on the Alter. The men looked shocked at my actions but made no advancement toward me. I was then approached by the lady at the door who had been talking with my wife. It was suggested that I reach out by phone to someone who might help me with my quest. This sounded logical to me so I telephoned my Aunt. I remember it was about midnight by then and after several rings I decided to hang up not wanting to wake up my Uncle. I do not remember where we ended up that night but we left the church and the next day I found myself at my Aunt's home. She entertained me for the entire day until my Uncle came home from work. He listened to me explain some of what I was thinking about my situation then he asked me "Chris, where are you from?" "Where is your home?" I thought for a moment then said, "I am from here, Mississippi." Then he countered that it was true that my older sisters were from Jackson, but where was I from. I thought again and replied that "I guess I am from Virginia." He did not say anything else but went into the kitchen; put together two sandwiches, put them into a bag and allowed me to leave. I went to our apartment then straight to Arkansas to see my older brother. I was exhausted and confused as a person could be. I needed time to rationalize all the information my mind was processing.

Within a few months I had lost my job and found myself at my brother's home in Arkansas. I was again trying to self-medicate with beer but could not relieve my racing thoughts. I ran through his kitchen door where my brother held me down until the ambulance arrived to take me to a hospital. I soon found myself in my first Psychiatric ward. This was my first step into the mental health system. It would not be my last.

As I lay in the stretcher, strapped down and coherent, I told the medic beside me to take me to the Baptist Hospital. I remember he seemed shocked and turned to my brother beside him and asked how I knew we were going to that hospital when he had just found out himself that that was our destination. I had never been to Little Rock, Arkansas before. When we arrived at the hospital I was put in an exam room by myself. I sat for what seemed like hours then my family was brought in and I could tell they were going to release me allowing me to go back to my brother's home. They were assuming it was the beer consumption that took me into a state of mania but something told me it was much more. I knew I could not just walk out of that hospital, I had to stay and find out what was wrong with me. I could no longer live the way I was living. I had no idea I would face these same decisions seventeen times over the next fifteen years or so. My journey had just started. If I had known this I do not think

I would have been strong enough to accept it and I might have found another way out. Thankfully my ignorance saved me.

I found myself the next morning in a padded room. There did not seem to be a door and nothing visible except padding. I did find a red button on one wall so I pushed it several times but had no reason to think anyone was alerted. I laid down waiting for whatever was to happen next. Sometime later a large man opened a section of padding and led me to a room that had two regular beds in it and that was all. I was shown to the eating area and sat down to eat. My brother appeared and sat down with me. He seemed both nervous and amused at the same time. I was eating an apple and was thinking about the fight between good and evil. I was trying to rationalize which side I was on. I do not remember talking with my brother during this visit; he eventually left me to my confusion. I stayed in the hospital for three days. I left with no shoes, no medication and no insight into my illness. Out of sheer high intervention, my dear sister from California appeared with her youngest child at the time. She found me at the bus stop at the hospital. She told me years later that she had flown in once hearing of my breakdown and was determined to see that I was properly cared for and not left to be preyed upon or get into a homeless cycle. She instinctively knew the seriousness of the situation. This was also the first time my reliance on other family members started to wane. I had just begun the natural process that those of us that live with mental illness must endure losses. The loss of relationships, finances, self-worth, our standing in our communities and family; this is a hard lesson to learn but it is a reality that must be embraced to heal.

I remember a harrowing taxi ride to the airport to pick up a rental car, my sister trying to negotiate a contract for a car to take us back to Mississippi, and I at the time walking barefoot in the airport lobby looking ominous. After hours of white knuckled driving by my sister, we made our way back to Mississippi where my wife was frantically trying to find out where I was and what was happening to me.

I convinced her to take me to Florida to my parent's home so that I could take some time to think things through and come back to my senses. She and a friend of ours drove me straight there. Along the way I was having visions of large organizations following us to do harm to us. I remember driving into the tunnel on I-10 in Mobile, Alabama thinking we would never come out the other end. My mind was processing information at an incredible pace but I stayed quiet and said nothing to my wife or friend, thinking if I told them my thoughts, harm would come to them. Several hours later we pulled up to my parent's home in Florida. I was left alone.

Within a week I was handcuffed in the back of a police car. I walked into the Starvin' Marvin store and walked out with two 12 packs of beer. I had money but that day I just decided to steal the beer instead. The police soon found me since I had parked the car sideways in my parent's front yard with the driver's door still open. My father rushed home from his job and literally begged the police to take me to the local mental hospital instead of jail. This would not be my last encounter with the law. They agreed, so off to the Psych ward we went. I was kept in isolation for two months. I had my daily shot of Thorazine along with whatever other lethargic medication they could use to quiet me. My wife was spoken to privately and told she was a young, attractive woman so it would be better if she divorced me and go her own way since I was going to end up in jail, hospitalized for the rest of my life, or die from my own actions.

She told me this several years later.

Dr. Scrotum
and Nurse Ratchet

This was my second hospital as an inpatient. I was upstairs, the only patient there. I sat medicated but defiant on one of the two beds in a room where the lights stayed on day and night. The tech sat in the room next to mine watching TV and wasting time. I was escorted to a shower periodically where a psych tech watched me shower. The time only got interesting when the doctor (I called him Scrotum) nervously came into the locked unit and gave me whatever shot of medication he wanted for that day. I heard the medication name of Thorazine for the first time in my life. I was hostile and could smell the fear on him. I was energized and could not come down from my mania. I spent over two months under these conditions and it was only due to my faithful wife that I was let into the general population. The facility on the lower level was upscale with a pool and a game room. Apparently, there were famous names of people in "rehab" there along with others who had the money for such things and a few of us that were just crazy. By then I had been broken but not defeated. It would take an afternoon concoction of an additional dose of Haldol, given to me by a nurse that would smile each time it was given, to put me out each night. We held groups where family members attended with us inpatients along with a facilitator. I found out a lot about the others but I believe they left me alone thinking I would become violent. One day I was escorted out to a waiting van, taken to a nearby hospital where I was given a scan of my brain. At the time, I knew I was going to my death by way of lethal injection as they put needles in my arms and a warm liquid went through my veins and settled in my brain. I lay there waiting for the poison to take effect. Later, after I was taken back to the ward, I tried to rethink what had happened but I was too numb from the medication. I would die many other times, it was exhausting.

By the time I got out of the facility all I wanted was a beer.

Once out of this hospital I was to go back to the same doctor for my Thorazine shots weekly but after a few times doing this I refused to participate in his care and turned back to alcohol. I did find employment for a short period of time but within a few months after getting out of the Mental Hospital, we were on our way where we started out a year ago, back to Virginia.

The Berlin wall came down (because of me)

I was in a chair approximately three feet from the TV watching it unfold. My nerves were feeling on edge. I was engrossed with what was happening. My eyes would close and my body would float above the chair, hovering in pure energy, positive energy that was being sent from healers across the globe. Goodwill was being sent out where the people knocking down the wall would receive the strength to carry on. It was humanity at its best and I was in control. If I raised my arm it sent a signal to the ones on the ground to do a specific deed. If I nodded my head it meant something else. It was a great responsibility; people's lives were at stake. I sat there orchestrating the event but was afraid to make one move that would be misinterpreted where someone might be hurt unintentionally. The world was changing for the better and I was the cause of it. All the organizations looking for me and those that had found me were at bay. I finally lay down in bed. My wife was asleep but I lay with tremendous anxiety hoping all went well. I started hearing nails being driven into wood. My mind raced trying to put reason to this. I suddenly realized "they" were building a hangman's structure. I did not dare look out of the window to verify my thinking, the building went on. Nail by nail, a pounding unmistakable. I lay in bed, eyes wide open until the sun came up, ready to go to my demise. I was afraid. They had finally gotten to me and now I was to hang. The sun came up; I cautiously went into the living room and ever so slowly peeked out the corner of the curtains. The pounding of nails had stopped, the sun shined through the window as I opened it so narrowly. There was no structure to be seen. All the noise and visualizing what was happening all night did not happen. I would have to revisit my thinking, make sense of the events of the night. I was ready to die, but not today.

Dark Days of the Nineties

We moved in with my dear mother-in-law who did not mind us moving in as long as we paid our own way with food and shelter. This was agreeable with us for we had no other place to stay now. My wife continued working and I began to drink more and more. I finally agreed to seek help at the Veteran's hospital in late 1989/ early 1990. I went inpatient for nearly three months again but this was a totally different experience from the last. I remember my wife helping me dress into a hospital gown being prepared to go into the ward and I thought this was a one-way ticket to my death. I was so tired and exhausted from my mind's activity and the alcohol consumption that I was willing to go and do almost anything to relieve the mental anguish. It was during this stay that I was first four-point tied down when I entered the facility. I did not remember this until I read my records during this period some 20 years later.

The first thing I remember was the smoking room. Now I was 29 years old and some of the veterans in this facility were much older. Some were prisoners of war and all had trauma in their past. There was a hierarchy both in experience and military rank that each held during their military service. The officers quietly ran the unit along with the enlisted with the most experience with mental health systems. I soon picked up that there was code being sent out constantly to each other by way of feet stomping, grunts and other signals to tell each member in the unit what they were to do next. It might be to leave the room, get a cigarette for someone or to simply stay put. I have come to believe this was the same code used in the prison camps during war. I was allowed after several weeks in the unit to go to eat a meal with the officers who were long term inpatients. It was amazing the respect they demanded and got in the "regular" chow hall at the hospital. I will never forget the quiet lessons of admiration and courage these men demonstrated, even when going through the mind-altering experiences they went through.

Once, during a chaotic time in the unit, the crowds of patients, including myself, were going wild. I do not know what started the commotion but everyone was running and screaming. I noticed that one of the leaders, a tall thin man, stood up in front of the front desk where all could see him and put his fingers down his throat forcing himself to upchuck in the presence of all involved. There was complete silence and we all went back to our rooms. Not a word was uttered. I considered this at the time and now to be the most amazing display of conscious thought and action I had ever witnessed.

I read a book written by a POW years later that touched on some of the things I witnessed in this ward. He wrote about being a prisoner of war where he had a rag to hold on to so that the long periods of time would go by without worthlessly letting your mind go as well. He would tie knots and count strings on his rag to pass the time. His rag had gotten old and frayed but he cherished it as a relief from the mind-numbing long extended hours upon hours of being confined. I took this idea of having something in my hands continuously whenever I was in mental wards years after reading this and it did indeed help with the monotony. This was one of my first coping skills.

Veteran's Psych Ward: 2-North

How could this guy I just met be Jesus Christ when I believed I was the chosen one? I was sitting in a small break room outside of 2-North (the inpatient unit) at the VA medical center when across the table a young woman was talking with and about a quiet man sitting next to her. My dear mother was sitting next to me. The young lady leaned over the table and said in a small voice that the man beside her thought he was Jesus himself. I heard them talk about this and that they were from 2-South, the other inpatient unit at the hospital. Now this confused me. How could this man be J.C. when I thoroughly believed at the time that I was the one with the world on my shoulders? I had just gotten permission to go outside the unit. My mother was with me as we walked outside and sat overlooking the bay that the hospital sits beside. It was a beautiful day and ducks were walking around us as we sat on a bench. I was trying to use my mind to tell the ducks what to do when I realized that my mother was talking. She was supporting me as best she could but I was too far into my world to show her the love I felt for her. I was controlling the entire world and it was heavy on my mind.

It was also during this time that the Psychologist I was assigned to had a meeting with my wife and me. He asked me a question that literally changed my life, although I did not realize it at the time. He asked me if I drank because I am depressed or if I am depressed because I drank. I remember thinking for a short period of time and answering him that "I drink because I am depressed." I was put on medication that was strong, Haldol if I remember correctly, but it took away the craving for alcohol I had for so many years. I believe this was one turning point for me since I was no longer suicidal or homicidal. It made me numb but the noises and voices in my mind stayed at bay. I would stay in this state of compliance for nearly ten years. I would have to go to the hospital many times more but for the most part I had quit drinking which had only exasperated my illness to the point of no return.

When I was released from the VA hospital after several months, I was still confused but I was manageable. A psychiatrist's dreams come true. I was compliant with my medication and was even able to get employed for a short period of time. My wife was pregnant and working as hard as ever. It was 1991 and I was working and we had our own apartment. I tried to stay employed but just could not work on a continuous basis. Our daughter Sara was born and soon after I was declared totally disabled by the Social Security Disability Insurance program. I did not even know this existed until a peer in one of my stays in a hospital told me to call Social Security and put in a claim. I did this and approximately 8 months later it was awarded to me. This money, along with my wife's steady working gave us the ability to live and breathe a little.

I assumed the daily responsibility of raising Sara while my wife continued to work. I say I raised her but the opposite is probably more accurate. Sara was a quiet, smart and loving child. I do not like to think what would have happened if she was any but those things. I was steady on my medication but still required hospitalization periodically. I would sleep 12-14 hours a day not having any motivation at all. I almost lost my wife and Sara more than once due to my inactivity and I do not believe anyone would have blamed them for wanting a better life than I, at the time, could participate in. Once my wife was simply painting a wall in our home and I was sitting in a chair, smoking, watching TV and I suddenly felt the need to assist her with the painting. I could not physically get out of that chair to help her. I sat there crying. I was in the stage of recovery known as "life is limited". This is where one feels as though there is no life after mental illness, so just accept it. Again, I did not know this at the time but looking back on this example and years of other examples makes it clear that I had no hope that things would get better. Just take the medication and maintain.

The illness engulfed our small family. It affected every aspect of our life. I stayed medicated and my wife and daughter were isolated, not knowing what to tell their friends at school or at work. My wife took care of everything to make our life bearable. She shopped, ordered my medication and laid it out for me to take the right portions, fed us and did all the things to make our home sustainable. We existed day to day but there was always a cloud of uncertainty, a tense air of the unexpected about to happen. I would explode with anger or implode with despair. Extremes of an unbalanced mind were the norm when my mind was not functioning in a healthy way. I believe Sara suffered the most. She saw me at my worst watching me being handcuffed going on TDO (temporary detainment orders) time after time. Outside of the home all seemed fine; nice house, nice cars, well-kept yard, a dog, but inside hell was the standard. What was Dad going to do next? Is it safe to come out of my room? Do I dare ask a friend over for a sleep over? What do I tell my friends' parents when they ask what Dad did for a living? Is he retired at 31?

A young girl should not have to ask these things of a parent but this was the reality we lived with. Sara found a way to cope with these challenges and excelled in school, she grew into a mature young woman who is both street and book smart. We are very proud of her as she had to fight demons most adults can only imagine. She, like my wife, is a rock and I count on her support in a real way. Sara is an old soul.

Over the next few years, I was admitted to as many psych hospitals as there were in the Tidewater area.

Straight-jackets and good times at the Institute

I had done the unthinkable; I broke the code on which button to press on the console panel located just within the window where the mental health techs sat. The button that unlocked the door that allowed all to enter or leave the facility. I reached over, pushed the button and it was Christmas time of year. All of us, except the ones that were too far gone to realize that freedom was in their grips, were free to move about the hospital. We passed through the door with high energy and adventure. Some of us got to the outside door but that was as far as we got. The techs found us one by one and escorted us back to the psych unit. A head count was preformed then I was singled out as the culprit that pushed the button. I was taken down, injected with a large amount of something that started my world spinning, held down until a straight-jacket was produced and promptly put on me. I do not know how long I was in isolation, strapped to a bed, but I had to pee very bad but could not force myself to urinate on myself. At some point and time, they unlocked the door, asked me some stupid questions, took the straight-jacket off, then put me back in the general population.

I did not venture near the window again.

Frequent Flying

I was a frequent flyer. I was in and out of one hospital so much that I saw it go from one mental health facility name to another. Nothing else changed that I could tell. The same furniture was there, the same layout, women on one wing and men on the other with the medication and nurse's station between. The Psychiatrist attending did change; no better, nor worse.

During one of my stays in this facility I met a man by the name of John. He was a man a few years my senior and the lines on his face showed many years of trauma. We shared some ideas on how our minds worked and this was probably the first peer experience that I can remember that I learned how one person could influence your life so much with one encounter. John had a pinky finger missing on one of his hands. I asked him what happened to his finger and he smiled broadly and stated he had pulled it off. He said he had broken it so badly that he simply removed it. I was contemplating this when he made a statement that is vivid in my mind to this day. He said "Chris, nobody can read your mind." He was looking at me with all the wisdom he had gained from living with a mental health concern, all the trauma (mentally and physically) that he went through and was giving me advice that made me stop for a moment and truly think about what this peer was telling me. In my mind, I would and could not speak out fearing others could "read" into my thoughts. I had acted accordingly for years not talking to professional and supporters alike, fearing harm would come to them or me. Now this man that I had met a few days ago was telling me something that changed my way of thinking. This one statement was so profound that it changed my life.

It was much later, after many years had went by, I gave a speech to my peers in this facility. I had been trained to speak about my journey and try to show others like myself that live with mental health concerns that there are ways to improve your life and not rely on the mental health system as much. The same furniture was still there, the same layout. The faces had changed but the dazed look that I carried for so long was there as well. During my speech, one large man insisted on standing beside me and leaned on me, I just continued with my talk. A psych technician was showing concern about this but I looked at him with a look of assurance that I was alright with this man putting his weight on my side. It did not bother me since I was one of them, a peer through and through. I had walked through the fire and understood those still in the burning stage. The first stage of Recovery: "impact of the illness", where we are consumed by the thoughts that nothing will follow our diagnosis, nothing but horror and despair.

It was a relief to hear that key turn for me to leave after my speech!

Planting a Seed

One hospital that I was in and out of was a progressive facility that had a program for recovery. It was here that I saw my first actual Therapist inside a psych ward. She took us into the community room and held a group. We all sat there medicated and somber when she wrote on a blackboard the good aspects and positive characteristics of people that live with mental illness possess. She spoke of us having insight, creativity, and intelligence beyond the "normal" person. I was shocked and inspired at the same time. I had never heard anyone talk about anything positive concerning living with a mental health issue, much yet a professional. It moved me in a way that I vividly remember. She changed my life even though it was years later that I realized just how much. A seed had been placed and it sat inside me for a long period of time, but it showed me that "change was possible" and that there were those around me that validated my thinking and beliefs.

There were many short stories to be shared from these confinements. There were characters and dangers. I saw the good in people and I saw predators prey on those of us that were truly so far gone mentally that they could not protect themselves. I heard screams, moans and laughter that were no humorous matter. The stories below are examples of these.

The broken door

I usually stayed in bed most of the time I was in a controlled environment. A fancy way of saying a psych ward. As I lay one day at the behavioral center, I heard someone running down the hall towards my room and then a large "BANG" as they hit a metal door that led to the outside courtyard where we would gather to smoke. My room was the last in the hall, next to the door in question. I was put in this room alone. One of the only times I did not have a roommate except when someone was leaving between someone else coming in. First, I was anxious and did not dare to move but after a few minutes I peeped my head out my door and the metal door was swinging wide open, verifying someone had run hitting the door; breaking the lock on it. In psych wards these doors are very well constructed and it was no small feat to break one so whoever put their shoulder to it was a determined individual. I stood before the door contemplating if I should try to scale the 10-foot wall surrounding the courtyard or simply tell a tech and have it fixed. It must have been winter since I distinctly remember it being cold. I decided to walk down the hall where the techs were and tell them the door was open. The techs checked it out and then began asking me questions on how it became open. I told of the running footsteps but that was all I knew. This set up a large commotion where we were head counted and eventually let out to the courtyard where we smoked for a long time in the cold until a locksmith was summoned to fix the door. After observing those around me I came to believe a new inpatient just arriving in the unit was to blame for the broken door. He simply wanted a cigarette before bed. Once the door was fixed I went back to bed but stayed awake. As I lay there, a young man came to the outside of my door and was arguing with an older man who I knew. The younger was determined to jump me and physically harm me for "ratting out" that the door was open thinking he would have scaled the wall surrounding the courtyard and escaped to who knows where. Usually escapees were caught in short order and brought back to the facility where they were typically put in isolation for long periods of time. The older man was using logic telling the younger one that if he did indeed jump my ass that cops would be in the unit in a matter of minutes and he would just end up in jail. As they talked I got up from the bed, went to my door and opened it in such a way as to invite the young man in if he wished, but for him to realize I had been listening to the entire conversation and it might be his ass that got beat. I heard footsteps this time of the two walking back down the hall to the main TV area. I had a sleepless night that night but I think the young man decided I was too large a man to jump.

The swinging chair arm

I could not sleep this night. This was unusual since usually I was given strong medication to force me to sleep mainly so the techs could have a restful and uneventful nightshift. As I lay in bed I visualized danger. Extreme danger was near. I got up and walked to the dayroom where two men were watching TV. I had not been up this late before during a stay, as I wrote I was typically out for the night so I do not know if it was the norm for this ward to allow inpatients to watch TV so late at night. What caught my eye next put chills down my back and still does as I am writing this. A third man was in the room behind the two watching the TV set. He was sitting in a chair jumping up and down with his weight. He had a crazed look in his eyes, one I was all too familiar with. The furniture in this room and throughout the facility was heavy and strong but this man had an arm half way off the chair. He saw me standing there but continued to pull and jump as much as he could to get momentum to loosen the arm of the chair. I knew if he got that arm piece off all hell was going to take place. I envisioned a blood bath of the two men watching the TV who would have never seen him coming at them and possibly the rest of us in the unit. I immediately went to the tech that was half asleep and banged on the window that separated them from the rest of us and demanded he remove the chair in question. He wiped his eyes and summoned a second tech to accompany him to the day room where the TV was and they removed the chair to the dismay of the one trying to break the chair. They also inspected the rest of the heavy furniture and then all went back to normal, whatever that was!

AHH, the energy

I stayed in the "life is limited" stage for over 10 years. When Sara turned approximately 9 years old I suddenly realized that I could not even communicate with my young daughter. My thinking was clouded and numb. This realization shocked me into the first action of advocacy I did for myself and those around me. I asked my doctor to take me off all medication. Surprisingly he agreed. This was the year 2000.

I immediately went into a manic state or psychosis. I felt energy for the first time in a decade and I loved it. The visions I saw and the insight I possessed were spectacular. I would walk in the woods at 2 or 3 in the morning with my dog with only the moon to see by. I felt at times like it must have been for Native Americans in the wilderness to have all your senses tuned into nature to just survive. I have been a Chief, a Shaman, even Jesus Christ himself. These were exhilarating times and dangerous times. For the most part, people left me alone and realized I was in a place within myself but others took advantage of me or physically challenged me. I did many erratic things even by my standards and I was admitted into more and more hospitals, never finding a concoction of medication to stabilize me. I was like a stallion on hype medication, too much energy to be dealt with. It was during these years that I experienced straight-jacketing, more four-point tie-downs, more long-term isolations and over medicating to the point of hallucinations.

Mania

I was manic and it was euphoric. I walked with the knowledge that all things in the world around me made sense. It all had meaning and that I fit in as part of this wonder of mother-nature. I had the energy of a horse and all my senses were overcome with input from anything that moved or smelled. I noticed the smallest details from my surroundings. Once I found myself walking with my father, we came to a stopping point at the end of a cull-de-sac when I looked up at the tree tops and an eagle came down almost to our touch. It had its wings widened to their full length, making a swishing noise as it slowly flew up and out of our sight. I did not even look toward my father or speak. He would not have understood anyway. I (we) just saw a miracle of nature and all he saw was a bird that got scared away. This is how we as people who have experienced the life changing, mind bending, wonderful insight into other worlds see that world. As extremes of emotion whether it is the low of not being able to communicate with those we love the most, or the highs of ecstasy that we feel to the depths of our souls. Fortunately, I have grown mentally to be able to "turn off" this impulse to return to mania. I certainly would love to have the energy and insight of those days but the cost is just too high. I have developed coping skills that allow me to enjoy brief moments of natural highs but then I purposely do whatever is needed to bring myself back to now, the present. I turn down the radio, I regulate my sleep, and I take time out to walk or just practice mindfulness. All these things assist me in balancing the worlds I walk in; and it is as it should be. I work, I play and I have wonderful relationships with those I interact with on a continuous basis. Now in my journey I feel fulfilled in most of my life activities. I just do not want to go back to the mayhem of my earlier days.

It was during this time I was watching the history channel and the commentator spoke of the Shaman and how they contributed to their communities in a positive way whether it was to advise the leaders of their tribes or take an active role as a leader themselves. He spoke of these healers as people that were visionaries and could foretell events to the benefit of their people. I watch this documentary with great interest for I saw in myself these same qualities, true or not. The insight I believed at the time I had that others just could not see, was what I considered a gift. Since others could not see the way I did they could not possible know why I did the things I did. These thoughts have stayed with me to the present. I had the opportunity to read a book of a man that professed to be a Shaman who performed ceremonies to heal the sick in this time and place. What struck me the most about this reading was that this man who did the feats of Shamanism held a day job working with the railroad. Now if this accomplished person who was described in this book could achieve so much and find a place in his community to fit in as a positive member, why couldn't I. A seed was placed in my mind that possibly, just possibly I could achieve more in my life than being a disabled individual who lived on the outskirts of my community, relying on services to sustain me and my family and not contributing my fair share of responsibility and work, giving back instead of being the receiver of services.

Night rides with my pony

Sometimes I could not sleep for days. During the nights, I did whatever my imagination told me to do. No reason or rhyme to my actions. Sometimes I would drive my car (my pony) around the Tidewater area as fast as I could without sliding in a ditch or spinning out on the highways. I would drive over 100 mph through the tunnels and bridges of the seven cities and I would not even consider where I was going. I knew the area well but not well enough to not get lost. I would find myself in rural parts of the area with no visible signs of where I was or on a road in downtown cities I had no business being in. I would stop periodically and would hear sirens going around me and sometimes I saw policeman trying to catch me but by pure luck I was never caught. I would not be driving now if I would have been caught breaking so many laws. I called these adventures "night riding" where I envisioned myself a Native American riding his pony through the thickets of trees and bushes. I could have killed myself or others doing this but fortunately I can write about it today.

My dog Misty

I had turned on the radio and lay on the couch feeling the warmth of the fire coming from the fireplace. I had just finished my nightly walk with Misty and I was energized. I was in such a state of bliss that I felt and desired to stay in this state of mind if I could, time was on my side. As song after song was played, I knew the DJ and others were playing them for my benefit. I was one with the radio and the songs being played was in such order that I could envision all the ones who understood my struggle were coming to my aid. The "Best of Tool" was playing and the song "Schism" blasted on the radio. As the lyrics "All the pieces fit" were flowing through my mind, I was taken to another world, a world where I was the master of all things. The DJ kept playing and I was in a state of elation. Mentally and physically I was engrossed in the music, "All the pieces fit" kept circling my brain as I lay stimulated to the point of seventh heaven. Song after song validated my thoughts of all things aligning. I stayed in this mode until the sun came up hours later. I finally sat up, took a long breathe, turned the radio off and wondered what I would do for the rest of the day. I also wondered how my wife had slept through all the noise and commotion I had made through the night. I realized that another day was upon me, the same as any day before it. I had another episode of euphoria but this time I had come down from mania and did not require to be hospitalized. I felt refreshed, I knew that what I had experienced was only a fragment in my life, that possibly all the pieces would fit for me someday but for now I had to get Sara to school. It was mundane, but necessary.

Another time, my dog Misty knew I was not well. We had just had our midnight walk through the woods adjacent to our home. I was lying on our bed with no covers on my body. The house was cold but my nerves were such that I did not bother to pull the bedspread up. Misty instinctively lay across my legs bringing warmth and love. These moments and many like them play on my mind at times. I want the energy and intensity that comes with mania but not the danger. The danger of losing reality forever; to being in a wonderful place in your mind but find yourself locked in a warehouse where you are abused and neglected. I found that there is a middle ground, where the two worlds that we walk in become one. A balancing of the mind that comes with hard work and tenacity. The educating of oneself on themselves and their interaction with reality as it is today. A rational thought process that is hammered out through the clouds of confusion and frustration. I saw the real world in visions. During these days, I was once confronted by two police officers and a crisis intervention person who was to decide if I was to go inpatient or not. I sat in my recliner listening to Sara play classic piano while these three-people stood in my home being indecisive on whether I should stay or go. My wife had summoned them fearing I was a danger to myself or someone else. She knew me well and made a good call for my anger was building steady and I was indeed a threat. I told the lady police officer how I saw the world in visions. She listened politely then commented on how well Sara played the piano. The intervention lady then asked me something and I grew angry to the point of putting all those present in a defensive mode. They handcuffed me and lead me to the waiting police car where I was promptly driven to one of the psych wards I frequented. At the time, I resented my wife having so much control over my life but I have since come to realize that she saved me from myself many times and I am very grateful to her for protecting our small family the way she did. It took uncommon courage to confront a madman but she knew me well and she somehow knew I would someday live to give back to all those that gave me so much. To grow from the insanity when I could not be trusted to becoming a rational person whose judgment is sound.

To Virginia with love

I was in rare form, I was the most influential person alive and everything I touched turned to gold. Literally turned to a commodity where anyone who was fortunate enough to get whatever item I happen to touch would instantly become wealthy beyond their wildest dreams. Since I am a giver I decided to touch everything in sight. When we stopped at the gas station just inside of Virginia located on 58 East towards Norfolk/Virginia Beach I took it upon myself to touch everything in the store. I opened the coolers and touched all the sodas, all the bagged chips, as much candy as I could before my poor wife finally got me back in the car to continue our travel to the promise land, Virginia. I had been triggered by something (anything) during our trip down south to visit family. It was always a trying time being with those that are distant for most of the time, only present during good times or when nothing is needed. Not there when you go bankrupt from mental hospital stays and the bills are piling up or when my wife got laid off and we had to sell the house to get out from under a mortgage. Not there when I was searching for meaning to this life and went from church to church until I gave up since no one wanted us to be part of their community. This man with one eye who could not hold an adult conversation because the lethargic medication would not permit his mind to process information fast enough, we were the outsiders who lived day to day with no positive feedback, only our own determination that one day we would become a functioning member of society not relying on disability checks to make ends meet. Eventually this turn around did happen for us but all the negatives took its toll. We laugh, we love, we converse but down deep we remember being the outcast.

Overdosing on Lithium

During 2002, I was stressing out due to family visiting our home when I took too many lithium tablets, much more than was prescribed. I think I thought that if I took another then another, then my anxiety would lessen and I could maintain my actions. After two or three days, the family member left and so did my mind. The world was spinning. My wife and Sara were in the car and I was weaving and darting in and out of traffic. Somehow, we pulled in front of the General Hospital where I stumbled out and began swinging my arms about as though I was fighting for my life. My wife got too close to me trying to assist me when I hit her. A man ran from the entrance to the hospital and eventually I found myself on a bed with tubes coming from my arms. My wife and Sara came into the room where I sat dazed and exhausted when I told them I might not make it and that to remember I loved them. I apologized to my wife for hitting her.

I slipped into my first coma. I saw demons coming through the piping and ventilation system of the hospital into the console where the nurses were. I had visions of terror but somehow, I was in comfort. I do remember my parents and my wife standing by my bed talking about my kidneys not working since I had not passed any urine the entire time I was bedridden. I also remember vividly talking to myself and imagining my wife and Sara coming to my aid and helping me mend my kidneys by concentrating on green. Within a short period of time I slowly came out of my coma when I overheard the nurse beside me tell a dirty joke. I smiled and I heard her say that everything was going to be alright. To this day, if I need a positive jolt of inspiration I close my eyes and envision everything green.

I was lead to a bathroom where I could feel the tension in the air where everyone was waiting to see if I could urinate or not. I peed for a long steady time. All involved were relieved. Now it was just rehabilitation to regain my speaking ability and walking. Within a couple of months, I was back; back to the mayhem of cycling up and down mentally. I did acquire a pattern of shaking from this event. My head and righthand shakes almost constantly. When those around me ask why I shake, I tell them it is simply from the medication I was on for so many years.

One morning
I couldn't get up

Another episode that took place not long after but was caused by the medication I took was a diabetic coma. The night before I had a craving for something sweet and found a gallon of chocolate milk. I didn't know it then but my sugar levels shot to the 600 range. No one had even talked to me about diabetes so I was ignorant to the real possibilities of death. I was in a coma for the second time within a few years but this time it was not self-induced. My wife tells me that she called an ambulance after talking with one of my mental health providers who suggested she should. I vaguely remember being put on a stretcher and transported to the local hospital where I went in and out of consciousness for the next week. This time I was in so deep all I remember was asking the nurses for more and more ice water, stumbling into a shower to clean myself after several days and then the never-ending shots of insulin and more medication. I was fortunate that I was weaned off the insulin shots after 6 months but still take the diabetic medication to this day.

By 2003, I was considered the terror of our neighborhood and with good reason. I did not harm anyone but my actions confused my community and we were outsiders. During this summer, I had an altercation with the principle at Sara's school. The police were called but I was let off with a warning so I did what every manic person would do, I went to a nearby beach and confronted a crowd of people who made some derogatory remarks concerning me and my appearance. A man came at me to fight and when I fought back I was pushed onto a metal pipe holding a metal trash can to the ground. My eye was severely damaged and I lost consciousness for a brief point of time. An ambulance was called and I was escorted to the hospital for immediate surgery which left my eye with a hole in the middle and no iris or color. After the surgery, I was taken to the Riverside Psych Hospital as court ordered by the courts.

This was a turning point for me for several reasons. During this stay I went to a hearing at the hospital where my wife, my attending Psychiatrist, a community representative and a judge were all present to decide if I should be sent to a state facility for a long period of time. I was still manic and did not realize at the time the stakes involved. They decided to keep me where I was for two reasons. The state facility had no open beds for me and my wife agreed to supervise my actions in the community once I left the hospital. My wife saved my ass again.

Another reason it was a turning point is that I was given a concoction of medication that actually stabilized me for the first time since coming off the heavy medication of the 90's. But this medication not only stabilized me but allowed me to think and reason. Fortunately, I was still able to contain myself a few months later when I went before the judge after a warrant was issued for me concerning the altercation at the beach when I almost lost my left eye. The judge put me on 2.5 years of probation with the same time waiting for me in Jail time if I disturbed or assaulted anyone else during this time. A good thing was the charges were misdemeanors and not felons, which I was ignorant of the difference at the time.

It was right after the hearing when I showed up at my new therapist's office.

I was starting to rationalize why and how I had come to this point in my life and realized that I indeed needed professional help other than just putting medication in my mouth and seeing a Psychiatrist every three months, or during stays in psych wards. I was rational enough to reach out to the Community Service Board where they cared for people like me who live with a mental health concern. I had not even considered the VA hospital for all these years since someone there told me incorrectly that I was not eligible to seek services there. I made an appointment with a therapist who became the lucky one to get the referral for one messed up individual.

Once I realized that this therapist was very serious about me attending our sessions, the next couple of years were a listening and learning events. She listened and then I learned. I carried a lot of baggage from my experiences over the years and I expressed this in crying, talking, and generally grieving from all the losses I had experienced along the way. Besides my wife and Sara, My therapist was the only constant in my life and she never let me down. She encouraged me to volunteer to heal and interact with others than just my small band of constants. She took me to my next stage of recovery, that being "change is possible". Once a spark was ignited, she recognized it and suggested ways keep the flame stronger and stronger.

I took her suggestion and attended a non-profit organization meeting. I was just attending as an interested party but they happened to need a treasurer (all non-profits need a treasurer, I later found out) and they all seemed to be looking at me. I must have been in a semi-manic state when I told them that since I had a finance degree and plenty of time on my hands, I would do it. There was jubilation that they finally found a treasurer so I found myself in another stage of recovery, "commitment to change". I had made my first true commitment to myself and others for the first time in over 15 years. I was petrified.

My Therapist

I am an educated man! I told my therapist between tears and sobs. Why could I not understand my own feelings, emotions, even my physical pain? She patiently validated my thinking but did not pressure me to take an action of change. This would come at my own pace. It was my journey to walk.

I stumbled into her clinic in late 2003, bearded down to my chest and with one eye blackened from a fight I had with a stranger during my last manic episode. When I say blackened, I mean I had surgery on my eye that took my iris and the color of my eye out totally. I felt and looked like an injured animal. I came looking for some type of reasoning as to why I acted as I did even when the consequences were so devastating.

At first my therapist was strict. "Why are you late?" "Why are you not here?" "We had an appointment and your still in bed?" "Get up and come in, we'll still have 30 minutes!" This was how we started. Direct, effective and needed. I would not listen to anyone on a consistent basis but when she spoke I knew I should respond, her I could trust.

I sat across from her for a decade and slowly went through all the phases of recovery. I did not know it at the time but later as I educated myself on my own illness and the recognizable signs of recovery, I could see how she guided me and allowed me to change, giving me the power to develop self-worth and purpose. But only when I was ready for the next step or challenge and when it came my time for change.

I had an epiphany

I was having some excess energy one day and was pacing our home when out of the blue I imagined a world where I would be accepted for the way I thought and acted. A blend of realities where my visions of color, peace and harmony were not the norm but were tolerated, even appreciated. My thoughts took me to believe I could walk in two worlds at the same time. One, being the world of realistic thought that society places on us at any given time in history, the norms of this time and place. The other being a world that transcends time and brings mystery, beauty and energy that does not come to those that do not live with a diagnosis. A world of Shamans and Visionaries. I came to the realization that a certain balance of thought was needed to accomplish this. I would have to work hard and be persistent in my desire to live a complete, even holistic existence. This thought stayed with me to this day. I am writing this and this is how I live today, within these two worlds in balance.

These thoughts were validated several years later while taking a peer education course where in one of the textbooks it was written that those of us that live with mental health concerns do live in two worlds and must adjust accordingly to live fulfilled lives. This confirmed my thinking on this and strengthened my resolve to stay focused and balance my worlds to become as productive and reliable as I could be. I now find it second nature to shift from one thought to the next in a healthy way. While my mind still "races" I can find creative ways to make good use of my energies. Where I was consumed with negative self- talk, I now stay in a positive mode and along with a strong support system to bounce my thoughts off and get collaboration that I am thinking correctly on whatever issue is at hand.

Treasurer duties

In staying true to my development both within myself and the community at large, I started my treasurer duties with all the energy I could muster. My wife taught me basic computer skills to keep track of monies coming and going for the non-profit whose purpose was and is to support and educate those of us that live with mental health issues and their families. I met several peers that dealt with similar histories as me. Some of my beliefs were validated and some not but I was learning as I went. These activities, along with the professionals I was seeing, had me moving in a good direction mentally.

Within six months of being involved with this organization, several of us peers were chosen to be trained in a new program being developed where peers would facilitate support groups among our peers. I spoke with my wife and my therapist concerning this and they were both very supportive, feeling I could handle the responsibility. I signed up and off we went to Richmond for my first education class in well over 20 years. It was late 2007.

It was a three-day training where we were taught how to recognize cues (both positive and negative) in support groups. What dynamics of group participation/facilitation to look for, and how to handle crisis situations. The training was taxing for me but after some emotional breakdowns where I was supported by my peers I did pass.

I was elated. During the training, I met peers from all over the state of Virginia. Some of the ones I first trained with are still friends to this day. I found comradery that I had not known since leaving the military service, a sense of belonging and purpose. The training was also my first indicator that I could be of service to others like myself. I could share what I had learned concerning the mental health system to benefit those that would listen. I was on a mission and it felt good.

When I got back from the training I approached my mentor and friend Sherry, who instinctively saw hope and potential in all the peers she came to know. She was the leader of the peer side of the non-profit I was associated with and she gave a peer named Eve and I dual duties of starting and maintaining local support groups for our affiliate. I found a community center where we could conduct our first group. We started off with me and Charley. I would pick up Charley at the group housing center where he lived. Charley and I would sit and talk about recovery and other life challenges for an hour and a half once every week. This went on for several months. Sometimes I would pick up more people that lived in the same housing, but it always seemed to be Charley and me in the end. Soon, Sherry arranged where we could meet at the Community Service Board. This was advantageous since so many of us got our services there and was familiar with the facility. I was picking so many people up at one time that my wife insisted I buy a SUV in place of my small truck so I could transport all my peers and not borrow her SUV each day we had meetings. The gatherings grew in numbers over the years until we had three groups a week going at different locations including the Riverside Behavioral Center where I had spent so much time at during the dark days of my illness.

In mid-2008 I was chosen to become a state trainer of facilitators. Along with two others, I was flown to St. Lewis, Missouri where we were trained to train other peers living with mental health concerns to facilitate support groups in their communities. I met many national trainers that conducted the training who showed energy and optimism that inspired me to want to do as much as I could to reach my peers in a positive way. I thought at the time, and still do, if I could catch just one peer and save them from spending time in the mental health system then all the hell and anguish I went through was worth it.

It had been approximately 5 years since I had my last mental hospital stay.

I came back from the training energized and focused. I had no idea that this mission I was on to assist my peers would turn into a calling, a life-long journey that would take me from disability to full time employment. I did know one thing though, I was tired of simply idling away time. Of staying in, "life is limited", stage of recovery. Either I was going to make something out of my life or die trying. I had heard that Social Security could pull your check for showing signs of full recovery but this didn't faze me. I had fought against the grain before and this time I would do whatever it took to re-enter into my community in a positive way. So, I went to work (as a volunteer).

Groups and more groups

I began organizing, training facilitators, facilitating and attending as many groups as I could. I got paid for the trainings so I was earning money for the first time in over 15 years. The money was not much and it was just a nicety, but it did validate what I was doing was valuable. My self-worth began to grow.

We started with the one group in the Community Service Board and over time, we began having 15-20 peers attending each week. These were wonderful times of sharing, crying, jubilation and celebration of achievements (as my friend Becky would say). We had many "old-timers" through the years. But the ones I concentrated on were the newly arrived, the ones seeking a meaning to life and how they fit in. The ones in the first stage of recovery, the ones shocked by the diagnosis, no matter when it was first given to them. The ones "stuck" in limbo where you find yourself questioning your own existence and if life is going to be like this forever. Those questioning life itself and, maybe, how to end this misery called living. It was and is my mission. To try and light a spark of curiosity that one might just see that "change is possible", that the world we see as those diagnosed does have its advantages. The therapist I encountered such a long time ago was right, people that live with mental health specialties are intelligent, insightful, and creative. It is up to us to show society that all is possible, even for those of us that have long histories of hospitalizations and trouble with the law. I believe we achieved this to some degree during this time. There was so much more to do.

We started a second group at the Riverside Behavioral Hospital where I was a frequent flyer for so many years. It was attended by up to 10 peers on any given night. It was strange being part of the recovery system happening at the hospital. More than once I walked a peer down to intake to be evaluated for inpatient check-in when we felt as a group that this was needed for the safety of the peer. Some were admitted and some not, but I felt the life and death responsibility that goes with leading and facilitating groups of peers. This was heavy on my shoulders but I felt the need and promise of such groups were so powerful I kept showing up and so did the peers.

I learned many coping skills from my peers in these groups, I learned what to do to control my condition and what not to do that exasperated the down side of a diagnosis. I learned to be on a sleep regiment allowing myself certain hours for sleep and staying on this schedule for the long haul. I learned mindfulness where one can alter their state of focus by concentrating on an object until peace consumes you. I also learned to trust again, trust those in my life that were positive influences and disengage those that were a drain. I was the facilitator for most of these groups but I received so much more than I gave. These groups saved my life, gave me purpose, and taught me how to interact with others again.

My Therapist, My Wife and Rob

All during this time I was sharing the daily walk I was on with both my therapist and my wife. They both were so important to my recovery that I can't go on with my writing without stopping for a moment and write about the enormous gratitude I have for these two individuals. It was My therapist who sat asking pertinent questions concerning my journey and slowly nudging me in a healthy way to make my own decisions. She and my wife both were patient and persistent in finding ways to bring me out of isolation and back into my community. I can't think of one incident when my therapist or my wife told me to do anything. They both let me find the answers as it should be, on my own reason, in my own time. As I grew stronger in mind and spirit, they simply stood by and allowed it to happen. I had gone from isolation to a peer community leader. I had responsibilities.

I conducted trainings both local and within the state of Virginia as I continued facilitating our groups locally. On one typical night, a big man in stature came in early and sat across the table from me. I introduced myself and the man did the same. His name was Rob. I did not know this at the time but my life was to change forever.

Rob had been advised to come to our group as a way of learning to facilitate groups so that he would be able to eventually do groups for veterans of the military. I did not know this at first but when we shared that both of us were veterans, we immediately found a bond that is strong to this day. It was Rob who suggested we start an all veteran's group near the VA hospital where I had been an inpatient so many years before. I had been away from anything military for almost twenty years by now so I was apprehensive starting a group of and for veterans. However, the more Rob came to our group, the more comfortable I became with the concept. I found a library on Mallory Street across the bridge from the hospital that agreed to let us utilize their meeting room once per week. We started our group during the day time and thanks to Rob, we were having anywhere from 4-7 veterans per group. So, I was facilitating 3 groups now a week along with traveling for trainings. I was fully engaged.

The man with one shoe

I took the Amtrak to Slidell, Louisiana to visit my parents who now lived there. I had done this several times before. Sometimes Sara would go along with me for company. It was good times that we shared together between my hospitalizations and erratic behavior. On this trip, my mother and I went to downtown New Orleans to sit and eat beignets and watch the tourist come and go along the streets. As we sat a man who was obviously homeless and a peer (lost mentally) walked in front of us in the street. I watched the man who had one shoe on and was carrying another for a while then I looked at my mother and stated that I could easily be this man, lost and all alone. She said that this would not have happened to me since I had family support. I wanted to correct her and say that I certainly had support from a few people i.e. her, my wife, my sister from California, and Sara but that when I first began my journey with the mental health system almost all my family suddenly disappeared, including six of my siblings. I just stayed quiet and let the moment go by but she seemed to sense my feelings when it came to family support. We have not talked about this again. I do not carry any hard feelings toward those that decided not to be a part of my life during these years, but I now decide on who I want to be in my life. I have that choice and I have put up strong boundaries concerning this. For those that are confused about this, it is all alright. I was confused for years and I recovered to the point of functioning in my community. You will be fine as well. I found support with those mentioned above and within my peers. The ones that have been to the dark side of life and truly understand where I have been and maybe where I am to go. These are the people I want on my side, not those that would put me on a train to who knows where. Those I do not trust.

Dr. V rocks my world

I was invited to speak at a gathering of interested people on Fort Monroe at the theater on base. Those attending were interested in what we as a non-profit had to offer for loved ones and clients of families and professionals. Two things stand out for me at this event that took place in the summer of 2009. I was growing stronger mentally and able to hold conversations with nearly anyone who wanted to talk with me but my physical life was deteriorating. I was nearly 400 pounds and my knees were starting to groan from the weight. The years of Depakote and other drugs had me gaining weight steadily since my last hospital stay in 2003. I could not fit in the theater seats. This was embarrassing but I mustered through the presentation opting to stand to the side throughout. The other more excited thing that stood out was I was introduced to a Dr. V.

She was one of the first people in my life that simply glowed. She was energetic, focused and intelligent. I grew to like her instantly. She asked me about our recovery groups we were conducting in the community. I told her I was a veteran and spoke of the all veterans group we were holding presently at the library on Mallory Street and I noticed this intrigued her. I asked her if it might be possible for a group meeting place to be arranged for another group to be held at the hospital. She immediately agreed she would check the availability of such a place and she also asked me to join her weekly Recovery Process Group held at the hospital. She told me the time and place and I told her I would attend.

My recovery was now on a fast pace.

Rob, my ace in the hole

I called Rob and told him of meeting Dr. V and asked him to accompany me into the group that she invited me to. I wasn't aware but Rob went to several groups at the hospital and knew the inter-workings there. I told him which room I was to go to and he knew the exact the room in mental health. He agreed to attend with me which I was very appreciative for since it had been so long since my last time being at the hospital. So, when the day came for the group, I parked in a large parking lot, made my way to mental health, and went to the window to check-in for Dr. V's group. The person behind the counter told me to go back to Benefits to have my eligibility confirmed and then come back. It was 15 minutes until group time so I just waited until Dr. V showed to open the door to the meeting room and slid in before the clerk saw me enter. Several other veterans came in, sat and casually made small talk until Dr. V took control of the group. We were having "check-in" when Rob walked in. My heart skipped a beat since I do not believe I would have had the courage to come to this group without Rob's support. As he came in Dr. V had a look of surprise on her face. I didn't realize it at the time but the group was by invitation only, only those screened by Dr. V could participate. I told her that Rob was with me, she did not miss a beat but simply welcomed him and the group began. I learned from this first group that healing took place here. Each of us shared what was on our mind and a healthy discussion followed, facilitated by Dr. V. Since by now I had been facilitating up to three groups a week for over a two-year period, I was amazed at the depths of thought she provoked from us veterans. She allowed us to share and support each other in a way that most groups only touched upon. These men trusted her and each other. Rob, having been in many support groups at the hospital, felt right at home and he added a dimension to the group that seems to put all the pieces in place for us to learn, share and grow. I stayed in this group for two years only missing a few weeks. It is where I truly started to heal, to begin another chapter in my recovery, to find holistic support of mind and body. I would enter the fourth stage of recovery, the "commitment of change" and then finally the fifth, "action for change". But first, I had to prove my eligibility - I could not just sneak in each time we had group. I went to Benefits.

I still had my VA I.D. from the eighties. A worn-out card with a random set of numbers assigned to me. This was 2009; twenty years later and many aspects of the VA system had changed including the I.D. cards. I produced my DD-214 which showed I had served for a little over 6 years in the USAF and made an appointment with my primary care physician. Approximately a month later, I had my appointment with a doctor who asked me which services I needed from the hospital. I told him all services including mental health. He sat and pushed many buttons on a computer and soon told me my next meeting would be a screening for mental health services. During our next group with Dr. V I asked some of the veterans what to expect from the assessment and they told me to act, sound and look as though I needed mental health or they would not let me in. Apparently, the system was so strained from veterans needing this service that only those truly needing assistance could get in.

I showed for the intake appointment with mental health as scheduled. My name was called along with some 5 or 6 others. We were shown which room to go to and wait for further instructions. Two young ladies entered the room and gave us a form to fill out. Was I suicidal, homicidal or both? I was starting to complete the paper work wondering just how sick I should appear when one of the ladies asked me who suggested that I sign up for mental health. I told her I attended the Recovery Process Group with Dr. V. It seemed like the waters parted and I was suddenly in, with no other protocol, they took me to the check-in desk, made an appointment with a Psychiatrist making it official that I could participate in Dr. V's group. No more sneaking into the group room.

From the first meeting on, Dr. V suggested the members of her group join my efforts within the non-profit support groups I was still facilitating. She soon found a meeting room for our veteran's group at night time on the hospital grounds. We started the group shifting our efforts from the veteran's group at the library in the community. It was a success from the start. We had those that attended our library group come as well as veterans that stayed in an inpatient program called the Domiciliary.

I continued training civilians in many parts of Virginia. I also started training veterans to facilitate other veterans that lived with mental health challenges. The first group of veterans I trained was a total of six with three being females. Each one of these individuals were special in their own way. And to this day I can still call on them for my support. We had synergy, the total of our participation and effect was greater than the individual parts that brought us together. It was amazing! With Dr. V at the helm, we started attracting more and more veterans. We easily had 18-20 veterans on our Tuesday night group and the business of recovery was always the topic. Once, a Peer Specialist that worked in the Domiciliary approached me and asked me why I put so much energy into the group. He stated that I would not get any return on my efforts such as employment or recognition. I told him to look at the veterans coming into the room as we spoke. I told him it made a difference to these veterans so it was well worth the effort. He did not get it!

As the veteran side of groups grew, I was being pulled away from the civilian side of things. We still had two groups a week being attended by peers. We did a local training for about 6 regular attendees who were to take over the civilian side so I could concentrate on the veteran program. This worked out well so I stopped coordinating and facilitating the civilian side.

Dr. V was our champion and I was the coordinator/trainer of our veteran's support group program. It was late 2009 and things were moving fast. Before long we had 8 groups a week in 3 different cities, all veterans helping veterans. I had trained over 40 veterans to facilitate these groups. A friend, Joe, once made a statement that we had a "Recovery Factory" and he was right. Dr. V had us attend one group a week just for us facilitators where we would discuss relevant topics such as facilitation skills and the dynamics of the groups we were facilitating. By now I had trained just about every veteran that was still attending the Recovery Process Group with Dr. V. This therapeutic group became a celebration of recovery. All of us, except some that were new to Dr. V's group, were feeling as though we were making a difference in our community of veterans. There seemed to be an energy that transcended the normal comradery of the veteran to veteran experience. We were helping veterans cope with long term mental diseases that had affected every aspect of their lives for many years, sometimes a lifetime.

It turned out that out of 11 Certified Peer Specialist at the VA Medical Center, six had been trained by me to facilitate groups during our program of support groups for veterans. Some of these were 100% Service Connected veterans who could have been penalized a portion of their disability for going back to work but decided it was the best move on their part for their own recovery. All these individuals gave many hours of their own time volunteering to facilitate groups with no agenda except to help their fellow veterans.

This insight and courage on their part can't be overrated. Even after horrific past trauma, they performed and still to this day in an outstanding manner. It was a pleasure knowing all these people and the rest of the ones that decided not to go for employment. I am very proud to call these individuals part of my support group and friends.

I advocated for myself

I had attended Dr. V's group now for at least one and a half years. Between this group and the volunteer work I was doing, I was feeling pretty good about myself. I felt that my contribution was making a positive affect with the veterans and civilians that I still trained periodically. I was contributing to the recovery of my peers and I found a calling in life that still guides me today. However, I was as heavy as ever and I realized I needed a change; a change in medication. My knees were getting worse and worse and I could barely breathe after any long walks or stair climbing. I spoke with my peers in Dr. V's group about this and they encouraged me to advocate for myself and change my medication if I felt so strongly about it. Now it might sound like a simple process changing your medication but I had been on the same cocktail for nearly 7 years and I was able to maintain and progress with my mental state all during this time. I was afraid as hell.

The next time I was with my Psychiatrist I told him my thinking and he agreed to slowly take me off two of my medications, Depakote and Cogentin. I would stay on Abilify.

After several weeks, I felt better than I have felt physically for many years. It was a success! I began losing weight and inches. This change along with being active was the key. My goal was total health (holistic healing), a goal I am still attempting to achieve.

Employment opportunities

My peer and friend, Sherry, who I was in close contact with due to our involvement with the non-profit we volunteered with, approached me with a job opportunity. She had held the position of supervising the peers and involvement with family members while working at the Community Service Board. She called one day and asked me if I would be interested in a full-time position working in the Crisis Stabilization Unit as a Peer Counselor.

I had considered employment before but after 20 years of being on SSDI disability I had to think very hard on this. I talked with my wife and my therapist, both were more than willing to support me if I did decide to take the position. After several sleepless nights, I called the supervisor who supervised the unit and asked if I could present my resume' to him. My resume' consisted of all volunteer work I had been doing for the last 4 years and my education I had earned as a young man. I filled a page so off to the Crisis Stabilization Unit I went.

I was granted access by a guard who appeared at the front door of the unit. I went in and asked for Dean, the supervisor. He soon came down the hall but before he got to me I had already viewed what was to be my working domain for the next 18 months. In the main area, there were comfortable couches and chairs for up to 10 clients (peers) at a time. A large TV which stayed on continuously, only turned off for time for group participation and bedtime. The nurse's station and crisis phone lines were overlooking this area. He escorted me to his office down the hall.

He read my resume' and agreed to hire me on the spot but I had to get cleared by his supervisor, a man named David. David gave me a call and scheduled a time we could get together. He met me in the hall of building 300 of the Community Service Board campus when he took me upstairs through a few coded doors then to his office. He sat in front of me and proceeded to ask me various questions about my qualifications. I felt at ease around him and he told me the one thing that he insisted on was that his employees should not and would not have any dual relationships with those we served. We were not to have relationships except for professional ones with our clients. I agreed to this and felt ethically fine with it. I soon found out why he would take this tone with me. Many in the human services field did cross this line and they lost their careers because of it. Within the week, I was in HR. I had my first job in 20 years and I was now a Peer Counselor.

The isolation room at the Riverside Behavioral Hospital

The Crisis unit was physically located adjacent to the Riverside Behavioral Hospital, a place I knew well from many hospitalizations there. A wing had been expanded from this hospital to make room for the crisis stabilization unit, which was operated by the Community Service Board. As I sat in Dean's office one day, I noticed that the layout was familiar to me. I had also noticed the line in the bricks on the outside of the building where you could easily make out where the building had been expanded to make room for the addition. It occurred to me that Dean's office used to be one of the two isolation rooms at the hospital. The other room next to Dean's office was utilized by the doctor that examined the clients. I was taken back to a time when I was isolated in this room for a long period of time and there was a young girl in the room next to me. She was screaming and crying out loud for several hours until she finally grew silent from exhaustion. I was quiet since by this time I was an old pro at being in isolation and I usually just laid down on the floor and sleep until the ones in charge saw fit to let me out. It seemed ironic that I would be in this same space and have my world totally different than my first encounter with this place. I did not mention this fact to Dean fearing that he would think it odd that I would make such a claim concerning his office.

74

January 6th, 2011, my first day as a full-time employee

I still weighed nearly 400 pounds but over the next 18 months I dropped approximately 60 of those pounds. The weight started melting off and continued for the next five years. I stayed busy taking the clients (peers) to the dining facility, outside for walks when the weather permitted and generally staying active. My job description was vague. I basically facilitated no more than two groups a day, performed individual and some family counseling, assisted in taking crisis phone calls, and did whatever I could do to be a part of the team. I had dual supervisors for peer support and Dean for day to day operations. I thoroughly loved my job. I was getting paid for what I had basically doing while volunteering since 2007. I still maintained most of my volunteering at the VA hospital and it was in my schedule that I could attend certain groups such as Dr. V's group and those held in the evening. I had a busy schedule but I was feeling as though I could maintain. Within a few months of being hired, I was accepted to attend the Certified Peer Specialist training in Georgia. Georgia had a reputation for being where Peer Support was organized and transformed into a profession. I was thrilled and apprehensive at the same time. The cost was over $1,500.00 for the training with room and board for two weeks which was money we didn't have. My wife was supportive as ever so we put it on the credit card. The only other issue was that I needed the time from work to go to this training. I contacted David who gave me his blessing to go to Georgia and they would still pay my salary for the duration. I was all set, I packed my bag and off to Georgia I went.

My eyes were opened to possibilities of true recovery

Virginia did not recognize the Certification of peers as a reimbursable service for those serviced within the mental health system. Georgia, however, was reimbursed by Medicaid for such services and they were instrumental in what is called, systems change. The changing of services from a "maintaining" of us peers to a "recovery based" system where recovery was not only possible but an expected outcome for each person served. I was one of 40 in the training to become a Certified Peer Specialist, CPS and the only one to be from another state other than Georgia. I found the concepts and theories that we covered amazing and practical in giving peer services to those of us that have mental health and/or substance use disorders. We studied and discussed things like; belief systems, negative self-talk, and the stages of recovery that I have been referring to so often during this writing. We touched on the Wellness Recovery Action Plan (WRAP) which is an evidence based practice tool to be used by us both with our peers and for our own recovery. I had been trained as a facilitator of WRAP a few months earlier under a mentor and friend Becky. This WRAP training was another turning point in my recovery where I had developed a plan for those times I needed support and for my daily walk with a diagnosis. I met many peers from Georgia and I am still connected to the Georgia Mental Health Consumer Network (GMHCN) today. It was stressful being in this training to be a CPS and there were times of tears but I passed the classroom instruction. I would have to come back to Georgia some two months later to take a written and oral exam. I made the trip with Sara who quizzed me on the material all the way down to Decatur, Ga. Besides the classroom instruction that amazed me was the recovery mindset of those attending the training. Some of these peers were in day programs where they would attend a structured setting throughout the day doing various social skills development programs to teach them how to basically get along with others and their support systems as well. These programs are usually for the lower functioning in our communities but in Georgia these same people were getting jobs, going back to school, living independently and generally recovering to a degree that they were finding happiness and fulfilment in their communities of choice. And not just a few but a large part of the population we are talking about. And those who were in my class of CPS's were in stages of recovery that to me seemed healthy and thriving. I left the training energized and with practical material to help me help my peers in the Crisis Stabilization Unit and my volunteer activities as well. I felt much more prepared for my next journey's chapter. I went to work for the VA Medical Center.

Being encouraged to apply

I enjoyed my position at the Community Service Board in all aspects except the pay. I was making less than $10.00 an hour and my disability check was cut many months earlier (which caused my knees to shake for several weeks). We were making our bills but I was making less money than when I was disabled but the benefits to working far outweighed the monies lost by working. My self-worth and physical well- being were so much improved from just one and a half years before that many in my circle did not recognize me at first sight. I had lost the 60 pounds but the inches I lost were more obvious. I went from a size 58 in men's pants to a 48 by now and I continued to lose at a steady rate. I felt better than I had in many years and the medication change I had done not only allowed me to shed pounds but improve my social skills. The working dynamics which I was not familiar with, after not working for so long, did not bother me as much. So overall, working is where I needed to stay, not disabled.

I continued my volunteer activities along with my work schedule, also attending Dr. V's group as well. I had found a comfort zone with the veterans in the group and they were encouraging me as I steadily walked toward a healthier life. As I mentioned before, most in the group were trained as facilitators so we all were becoming mentors and leaders in peer support. I grew very fond of these men and women, who gave so much of their time and energy trying to help others like them; manage and grow in recovery.

Mamie's funeral

Mamie was a classy lady who had overcome and dealt with a lot of trauma in her life. She facilitated veteran groups along side of me many times and she showed me what courage was all about when she attempted to put a support group together in the community living center at the VA hospital where she lived to her final days. I visited Mamie approximately a week before she passed away. She took me to her room in the living center, sat down across from me and began telling me of her ungodly trauma that she had been through. She spoke and removed her head scarf as she told me her journey. Her hair was gone from treatment, but to me, she had never been more beautiful. She spoke of the trauma as the reason for her cancer. She talked about the evil and negative thoughts that she was combating on a continuous basis that had grown within her and had gotten to the point that it became fatal. I sat crying listening to her, remembering the energy she possessed just a few weeks before and all the time I had known her before this day. She spoke of how Dr. V visited her every day and would spent time with her. She was so proud that Dr. V had done this. I do not know if she even recognized my tears streaming down my face as I watch her glow with life, even as hers was about to end. She asked me for a new facilitator's guide that we used in groups so she could start a new group for those in the community center that needed support. This was classic Mamie. The next day I went by to give her my personal guide. I left it with a nurse. I do not know if she ever got it.

When I received word of her death, I approached Rob to see if we could go together to the funeral. He agreed, so the following is what I remember. I wrote a letter of the gathering (funeral) to Dr. V detailing what I witnessed. I do not know if she still has the letter but I will try to bring you (the reader) into my mind as best I can.

Rob arrived to pick me up from my home in Chesapeake, Va. He was dressed in a dark suit and took on an air of reverence. I would often call him my righteous dude. We arrived at the funeral being held in Norfolk a bit early but still had a hard time finding a parking space. People were streaming into the church from all sides of the front. We were greeted by several men ushering each person into various parts of the church, we were shown to a viewing room outside the main pew area. We could see everyone but a glass partition kept us from hearing everything that was said as those in the front podium started to move about. A man came into our room and turned on a TV in the corner and adjusted the sound where all could hear. A friend of the family stood at the podium and read a note from Dr. V to Mamie's family. This was done with great anticipation and theater. The writing was well received by the family and those in attendance. It was obvious to all that this (Dr. V) knew Mamie well and as it was read we could see various people in the crowd nod and cry out, dance and sway.

A man, who I believed was Mamie personal pastor, gave a sermon like I have never heard before. And as he jumped, yelled, cried and shouted, all of us present began doing the same. Soon other healers would join in. It was truly amazing to witness such a celebration of life. This was no funeral like I had been to before or since. I was so moved by the experience that I sat crying and swaying. Rob leaned over and asked me if I was alright. I simply smiled and nodded yes. At some point in the event, Rob stood up and motioned for me to follow him. We left the church before the burial was to take place.

I felt refreshed in this human experience. I was uplifted and only thought goods thoughts concerning Mamie's life. How she was surrounded by those healers in this church she attended regularly. How she had helped others with trauma that spoke at her funeral. She was a giver even though she had been through so much. I knew her as a veteran and as a facilitator of support groups; they knew her in her intensely private and vulnerable states. They sheltered her from the storm of life. Now I knew where she drew her strength from. Her community!

We went live from
the Veteran's hospital

Dr. V put together a Webinar where we would share what we were doing in our VA hospital with other interested parties across the country. We sat around a microphone and presented our program then responded to questions from participants of the Webinar. Presenters were me, Dr. V, Sherry and about 10-15 of our facilitators. Now this was a big thing for me and I suppose, to the rest of us involved. We spoke for about 50 minutes then answered questions from those on the line. It showed us just how much our program was getting noticed. It was uplifting for all involved. I was getting grant monies to conduct the training of more veteran facilitators. We grew until we had three possible facilitators per group. Dr. V had moved us from inception to an organization, making recovery a system wide movement. One could tell by just being in the halls of the hospital that it took on an air of possibilities. The veterans in the waiting room in mental health were talking, smiling, and socializing. Not sitting with their heads down and lost in their own worlds. We were making a difference one veteran at a time. It felt good. We continued working; this was the year 2012.

Not long after the webinar a position for a Peer Specialist opened at the hospital. Dr. V let me know it was open and encouraged me to apply for it. I did know most of the people in mental health and I could use several of the doctors there as references so I decided to apply. I had the right credentials by then; being a Certified Peer Specialist (CPS), being a veteran, having worked at the Crisis Stabilization Unit for approximately 18 months, and having been a volunteer for nearly 5 years. I got the interview but before I sat for the interview, Dr. V told me she had to excuse herself from the interview process due to our close relationship. I understood the reason for this but it gave me an air of uncertainty going in. I showed up early and wore the only sports jacket I owned. I was shown to a small office with four VA employees present. They took turns asking me about 8 or 9 questions. I knew two of the interviewers personally but the others I had to ask who they were and what positions they held in mental health afterwards. I thought I did well but I did not know who else applied or were interviewed. Peer positions are very competitive since the requirements for these positions were minimal at the time. Peer services has grown a lot during the last five years or so, mainly due to many forward-thinking peers that have influenced the system that we worked in.

I got the word that I had gotten the job at the VA when I received a call from HR at the hospital. I accepted immediately and gave my two-week notice to the crisis stabilization Unit. Dean, David and the others seemed sincere with their good wishes seeing me off. It would be an adjustment for me and new working dynamics, but it did solve one thing I found lacking at the Community Service Board, I would earn a livable wage.

From Inpatient to Employee

I was in orientation at the hospital when I looked at my new fellow co-workers and thought of my journey from inpatient at the hospital to full-time employment. Mentally I was feeling good and physically I was continuing to shed weight. I found out that I was being assigned to the homeless program named Housing Urban Development/ Veterans Supportive Housing (HUD/VASH). I was to be the only peer specialist assigned to this program. I had an extensive background in mental health and substance use disorder but homelessness and the section 8 program dealing with housing vouchers was new to me, I was apprehensive to say the least. But I was no longer receiving a disability check so it was a matter of putting the food on our table at this point so I went to my new working station at building 71 and put my best foot forward. When I presented myself to my new supervisor, I felt immediate warmth from her that put all my fears aside. Linda was a bundle of energy and enthusiasm. She welcomed me with open arms and soon I became settled into my new position. Within a couple of months, a new peer was hired to work at the hospital as well and he was temporarily placed in our building so that I could mentor him. This peer was the first one in the profession of peer services that I had met that did not believe in recovery from mental health or substance use disorders. He was a former psych tech that triggered me into a state of mind that was unhealthy for me. In my mind, psych techs were the ones that held me down and injected medications that took me to the vegetative state. I stayed as far as I could from this individual and he eventually went to another program at the hospital. This event strengthened my recovery by letting me know I did have limits and that recovery is not a linear process. We do have setbacks and at times, are tested but I managed to grow from this and (I think), evolve into a stronger peer because of it.

I was proud of my work with the homeless program. However, after 2 years I just couldn't keep up my duties on the job and my volunteer position at the same hospital. I decided that I had to let the volunteer program go and quit as coordinator and trainer of veterans for the non-profit I was associated with for seven years. I shed some tears having to do this but it freed up so much of my time and energy that I feel it was the right time for this.

During the seven years I was associated with the non-profit organization. I had trained or helped train well over 100 of my peers (both veterans and civilians), become facilitators of support groups for our peers. I had facilitated or co-facilitated probably over 1,000 group meetings. I had come to know many of my peers as friends and fellow travelers in this life. I now chose who I wanted in my life. I sincerely appreciated these individuals for their support and encouragement during this time and now. I started volunteering as an isolated person trapped in the mental health system then evolved into a whole person with insight, coping skills, and a support system that sustained me over the years.

I continued to work at a steady pace within the HUD/VASH program and I believe earned the respect of my co-workers and the veterans we serve.

I stayed at this Veteran's hospital for nearly five years.

One day, my wife told me her company that she was employed by was showing signs that a lay-off might be coming. She had been let go two times in the past so she knew the indicators that this might happen. We discussed our living situation and how we wanted to live into our later years so it was decided that I would look for a transfer within the VA system to another peer specialist position. The place we both agreed on was Florida as the only state besides Virginia we both wanted to live in so I began a search for open positions.

I found four that fit my pay status and job description, so I applied for all four. I received interviews on two of these, Tampa and Orlando. I was accepted by both but had to decide which one to choose. After talking with my wife and weighing everything concerning the move, we decided to accept the position in Orlando, Florida.

I was apprehensive to say the least. For nearly 30 years we had called Hampton Roads our home. I had evolved from a diagnosed man who had a limited life, consumed by my mental health illness to an individual who was accepted in his community and who saw the opportunities in life and not just the shortfalls. I had learned enough that I could function at a high level in probably the most demanding of all professions, that being human services. I had been educated not only on my own illness but in the proper way to assist my peers to meet their own potential according to their wants and desires. I had worked full-time for nearly seven years, which after the first year I was taken off Social Security Disability, and was earning a livable wage. I had become the main wage earner in our home and it was very good for my self-worth. I had found a balance in my two worlds that I wrote about earlier. I was so adapt at practicing my coping skills I had learned from peers and trial and error that it was like I could maintain my mental health effortlessly. But of course, it is not quite so easy and it took many years of mind-bending processes to come to the point that I could function in today's reality. One of the hardest things I had to overcome was the daily dynamics of my work environment. When I was disabled, I was free to tell whomever I wanted to stay out of my life but when you must show up day after day and deal with the same co-workers, it requires skills that I had lost many years before. To this day I still take mental wellness days off to regroup and recharge for the next time. Fortunately, I have had four separate supervisors who were all wonderful in their own way. As it is said "No man is an Island" and I depend on others in my support system daily. This support system that I had developed after so many years in Virginia was what I was so afraid of leaving when we decided to move to Florida. I have since found that by having e-mail and phone contacts, I have been able to maintain a strong support system even with 800 miles between most of those I count on.

I attribute my mental health wellness to having learned these traits I write about; coping skills, support systems, knowing oneself to the point of knowing when you get triggered by something or someone, knowing when "things are breaking down" and when to seek help. All these things contribute positively to my state of well-being. All those peers and mentors in Virginia who helped me along my journey to this point are angels to me. I just hope I can give back as much as I have received in assistance from others.

Off to Florida on
a wing and a prayer

So off to Florida we went. I had to be at work earlier than I would
have hoped so I went south a couple of weeks by myself then returned
to Virginia to sign for the house to be sold and get my wife, who
had to terminate her position at her work. The move was a risky one
on our part since my wife had no prospects of employment, we had
very little cash on hand and I was coming to unknown territory
concerning my position. I was familiar with the Florida lifestyle
though having gone through my high school years in Jupiter, Florida.

It felt good crossing the Georgia/Florida boarder for the first
time in many years. The Palm trees were a wonderful back drop
on I-95. The last time I spent any time at all in Florida was when
I was inpatient at the Psych Hospital. I was now coming back as a
full-time government employee with over 10 years of service time
(military and civilian). I earned a steady check and more important
I was proud of the profession I chose to work in. I honestly feel as
though I was making wise decisions, healthy ones that served both
me and my family well. Mentally, I felt strong and I had by now lost
well over 120 pounds since I began working in 2011.

We temporarily lived at an extended stay near the airport and started our home search in earnest. I qualified for a small home on my own income so we looked for a home in this price range. The market was brutal. It took approximately five contracts before we secured a home, after 2.5 months of searching and waiting. My wife was looking for employment the entire time and soon landed a job with a large Credit Union. We had our furniture delivered in August of 2016 and settled into our new surroundings.

Except for the housing search, all went well as far as the move went. I should not even complain about the home front either since we did find a suitable home in a nice neighborhood that fit my wife and I well. My job was a nice change from being at the main hospital in Virginia. The atmosphere was more "laid-back" since our main hospital was over an hour away. The work is concentrated on customer service and doing what was best for the veterans we serve. I enjoy this and am encouraged to do my work in a way that made sense.

I had by now been working in the homeless program for nearly five years and I continued to enjoy this tremendously. I thrive on assisting veterans who require a "hand-up" when they need us the most. I felt great pride in seeing a difference we make each day in these veteran's lives. My job is very diverse but there is one constant, that being I am invariably sharing what I have learned in my life concerning recovery. A simple trip to the hospital can turn into a life- long learning experience for both the veteran and myself. My job is to model recovery and share my story when effective. You can't ask for a better job than that!

When we are no longer able to **change** a **situation,
we are challenged to change ourselves**.

Viktor Frankl

Out of the five steps of recovery, three address change. The third step being "Change is possible", the fourth "Commitment to change" and the fifth step "Action for change". Before I had learned these concepts of recovery I had not given much thought to just how much change we must undergo to live a balanced life. The quote above was first derived by a man who had undergone the horrors of the concentration camps in Nazi Germany. I can only imagine the strength and change it took to survive such a dreadful time.

When I was at my lowest point in my life, I could not rely on my mind. My confidence was such that a trip to the store was unbearable. I stayed isolated for many years, relying on my wife to counter the reality I could not face. I do not compare my situation with that of Mr. Frankl, I am just trying to convey that we that live with a mental health concern are in a war within ourselves. We must overcome adversity in our own minds where our chemical imbalance overshadows all thought processes. Where negative self-talk becomes the norm and we can easily fall into a vegetative state.

As I lived for 15 years in the second stage of recovery, where "Life is limited," I had no idea that "Change was possible." I am a fortunate person for I had support from certain people in my life that sustained me until I could change for the better. I could have easily drifted into poverty and perished either by my own hands or some other way. My options were limited since my mind had "shutdown". I try to look back at these times and recall just what I was thinking but the lethargic medication I was taking at the time clouds my memory. I believe each of us wants to contribute to their community of choice, but it is hard to engage others when your mind is telling you that "they" want to do harm to you or those you love. The paranoia is a real fear, not just a symptom or condition.

I had a long time to rationalize my thought process which I know is not the case for many others who are trapped in terrible relationships, are trying to put food on the table, have children to raise and have a multitude of other responsibilities to contend with. I can empathize with these individuals but even with all the challenges I have had with my mental state I still consider myself one of the fortunate ones.

I was recently riding in a car with a co-worker and we encountered a young man who was not doing well with his mental health. He had no support, family or otherwise. The only link he had with support was us, his mental health workers (the system). He had no money coming in and was in bad physical health. We offered what resources we had and attempted to assist him in getting services. It occurred to me that this man reminded me of myself in many ways. I turned to my co-worker and stated, "This young man is me without my wife, that if not for the support I had from my wife keeping a roof over my head all those years I drifted mentally, I could have easily been in this man's shoes."

Therefore, I write that I am one of the fortunate ones. Even though I might have been in harm's way many times and have been an outcast to my community, I was able to have the precious time to make that change I needed so badly. It took many years but I eventually made that turn toward holistic health.

After Thought

As I am writing now in the present tense, I am reminded of just how far one can go even living with a mental health concern. I have friends (peers) in my support system who are true trailblazers in the peer movement. It can't be stressed enough how important it is to surround oneself with like-minded people who cherish their sobriety and healthy mindset to a degree of not returning to the dark days. I honestly can't say if I might be triggered by an event that will tear at my soul, but I have tools in place to catch myself (hopefully) before I get too far into the other world with no returning to this one. There have been great strides in the mental health systems to date and more needs to be done. Peer support is just one pit crew member on a team of disciplines that support the driver of services, the one being served. Person-centered care is being recognized by more and more professionals as the key to humane and effective treatment. The outcomes are better and there is even cost savings. But beyond this, it is the right thing to do!

There are still those though in the human services field that would lock us up in warehouses and feed us medication to "maintain" a sort of control over us but as I have worked in the field for over 7 years and volunteered 3 years before that I have seen doctors, social workers, nurses, peer providers and volunteers work tirelessly trying to shore up mental health systems that are cracking from underfunding and lack of personnel. I have worked in civilian, state and veteran systems and across the board what I have witnessed is uplifting and inspiring.

Peer support services is assisting in this workload disparity with good results but our culture must be changed to have lasting effects on the stigma that is associated with us that carry a diagnosis.

I am compelled to write directly to the young ones. Not necessarily the youth in age but the young in recovery. As you educate yourself on the possibilities and probability of a quality life (as you define it), please remember that the losses you have endured will make you stronger. We that live with a diagnosis have lost finances, friendships, family, the standing in our communities and sometimes our self-worth, but we must look beyond these losses and recognize that recovery is not just for a few but is the expectation. It is not the exception but the rule. There are those around you that can mentor you, support you, and help you heal. There are angels everywhere and it is up to you to recognize this. There are professionals that will hold the hope for you but there is also a matter of self-responsibility. Taking the consequences for your actions or inactions; I can only speak for myself and my recovery but there are universal theories and principals that guide us in recovery. Again, as you educate yourselves on these concepts, it will be clear to you that much thought and work has been done to assist you in recovery.

The five steps of recovery are one example of peers and scholars taking the lead in this education of us. These steps are basic but life changing. Entities such as SAMHSA are full of recovery based information that will help you better understand our illnesses (and strengths). They will even ship items for free! Another concept and practical application of thought is the "Eight dimensions of Wellness" also championed by SAMHSA. You can visit their website if desired.

With the age of instant information, it is as it should be - available to all of us. But rest assured that even with all these ideas and publications it still takes a curious mind and effort on our part to embrace these self-help materials.

What I am attempting to convey is the practical side of mental health. We Shamans and Sages envision a world where all exist to co-inhabit this world that we find ourselves living in. We must also embrace the world where there are haters and those that would take advantage of the vulnerable ones. We must look at "reality" as seen by others and find our place in this world.

My sister in California, once told me about "Living in the now". A sort of perpetual mindfulness of not worrying about the past or concentrating too much on the future but taking in the present and being truly present, making the most of this very moment. It might be a simple act of kindness or focusing on an item of interest to ease your mind. It might be to take a walk or call a friend for support. All these coping skills matter! They may seem simplistic and ineffective but in my life, these same types of skills have proven to help me go beyond the straightjackets, four-pointing, isolation and overmedication to a place where I am comfortable in my own skin.

When I went back to the Psychiatrist that I was under treatment with during the 1990's, during my decade in the "fog," I presented myself in a professional manner. This was 2016 and I was by now a professional in the same service he had practiced in for many years. I wore a sports jacket, was clean shaven and approached him with kindness and pride. I needed a Psychiatrist for my medication management since I left the service of another doctor. The encounter was strange to me at first. I was taken aback to a time when he made all the decisions about my care. There were treatment plans and goals written that I was never asked a single question about. A one-sided relationship where he possessed all the authority and power to have me go about my business or be locked-up for life in a state facility. I noticed he was feeling a little uncomfortable with me now that I looked at him square in the eye and met his questions with questions of my own. He was stating that I was truly sick before and his treatment was necessary for my own good. I acknowledged that he saw me through some dark days but that the insight I now had concerning my mental condition was after a long process of recovery, not just medication. He asked what medication I was taking now and I told him. It was far cry from the Thorazene, Haldol, and such that he had prescribed for me for such a long period of time.

He hesitated then wrote out the scripts I asked for. He knew I had come with options; the option to see him again (if he allowed this), the option to go to another doctor, or the option to simply not go to any doctor at all. Now it was my choice concerning my care, the way I see things, the reality as it is, we all have choices. We can choose to change for the betterment of ourselves, our families and our communities or we can choose not to. But rest assured it is your choice.

Just as I "chose" to stay at the Psychiatric Hospital in Little Rock, Arkansas many years ago to find my truth, I hope this writing has left you with a seed that might create at least a small change in you. I might be unrealistic about how one piece of literature can move a person, but I began this adventure with high hopes that I could make a difference in just one individual.

Perhaps that person is you!!!